CELTIC
Stained Glass Pattern Book

Mallory Pearce

DOVER PUBLICATIONS, INC.
Mineola, New York

Copyright

Copyright © 1999 by Dover Publications, Inc.
All rights reserved under Pan American and International Copyright Conventions.

Published in Canada by General Publishing Company, Ltd., 30 Lesmill Road, Don Mills, Toronto, Ontario.

Bibliographical Note

Celtic Stained Glass Pattern Book is a new work, first published by Dover Publications, Inc., in 1999.

DOVER *Pictorial Archive* SERIES

This book belongs to the Dover Pictorial Archive Series. You may use the designs and illustrations for graphics and crafts applications, free and without special permission, provided that you include no more than four in the same publication or project. (For permission for additional use, please write to Permissions Department, Dover Publications, Inc., 31 East 2nd Street, Mineola, N.Y. 11501.)

However, republication or reproduction of any illustration by any other graphic service, whether it be in a book or in any other design resource, is strictly prohibited.

Library of Congress Cataloging-in-Publication Data

Pearce, Mallory, 1935–
    Celtic stained glass pattern book / Mallory Pearce.
        p.   cm. — (Dover pictorial archive series)
    ISBN 0-486-40479-X
    1. Glass craft—Patterns.   2. Glass painting and staining—Patterns.   3. Decoration and ornament, Celtic.   I. Title.   II. Series.
TT298.P43   1999
748.5—dc21   99-14046
                                                                                    CIP

Manufactured in the United States of America
Dover Publications, Inc., 31 East 2nd Street, Mineola, N.Y. 11501

Publisher's Note

Celtic myths, lore, and artistic legacies are well represented in this collection of 91 patterns for stained glass projects, which reflects the traditions of the multitude of Celtic tribes that flourished throughout much of Europe during the pre-Christian era. After the Roman Empire conquered the Celtic peoples in all but the northern parts of the British Isles, the motifs of Celtic art were transmitted as folk art. This selection of patterns features many highly elaborated images of animals, of the kind that proliferated in Ireland during the Celtic Revival of the early Middle Ages.

Included are sinuous snakes; a fish; a rich variety of stylized birds and four-footed animals with elongated, interwoven, tendril-like limbs and tails; and symbolic representations of the Gospel authors Matthew, Mark, Luke, and John. Accompanying them are dozens of traditional interlocking patterns, in both flowing curvilinear and angular geometric styles, within circular, oval, and rectangular frames. The designs show a variety of influences—including the Etruscan, the Scythian, and the Greek—on early Celtic art of the Hallstatt culture (centered in what are now Austria and southern Germany, before the fifth century B.C.) and the later brilliant development of the La Tène culture in Switzerland. They range from linear designs for the decoration of flat surfaces to designs that create three-dimensional effects.

These patterns will be useful to craftspeople at all levels of experience. Those who are novices at selecting and cutting glass will want to use this collection in conjunction with an excellent instruction book, such as *Stained Glass Craft* by J. A. F. Divine and G. Blachford, Dover Publications, 0-486-22812-6.

1

3

4

9

12

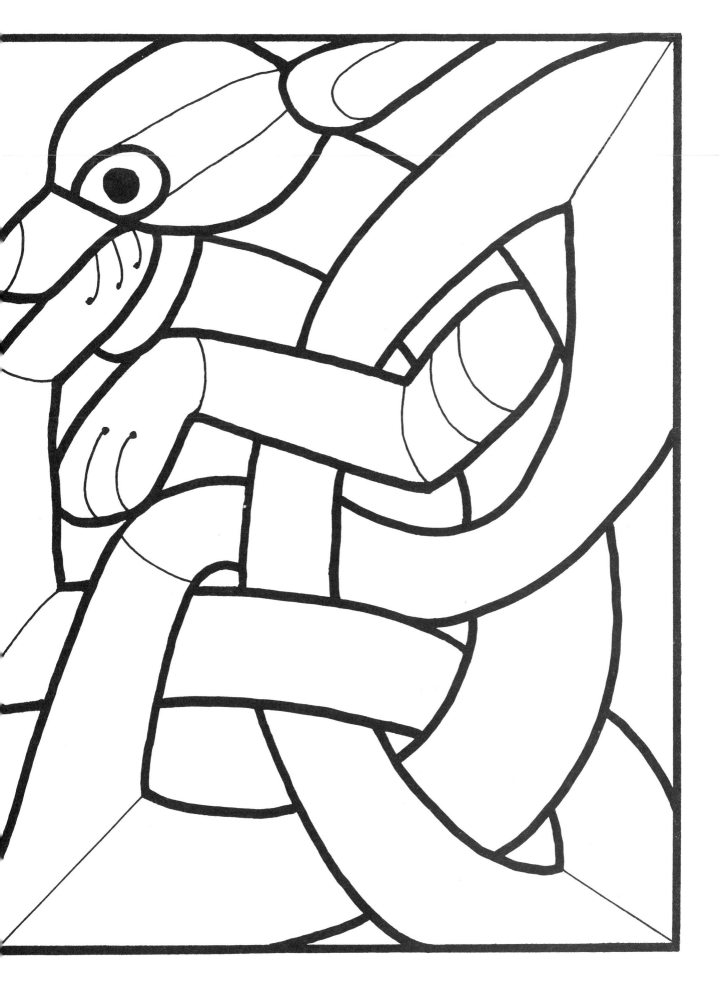

15

16

19

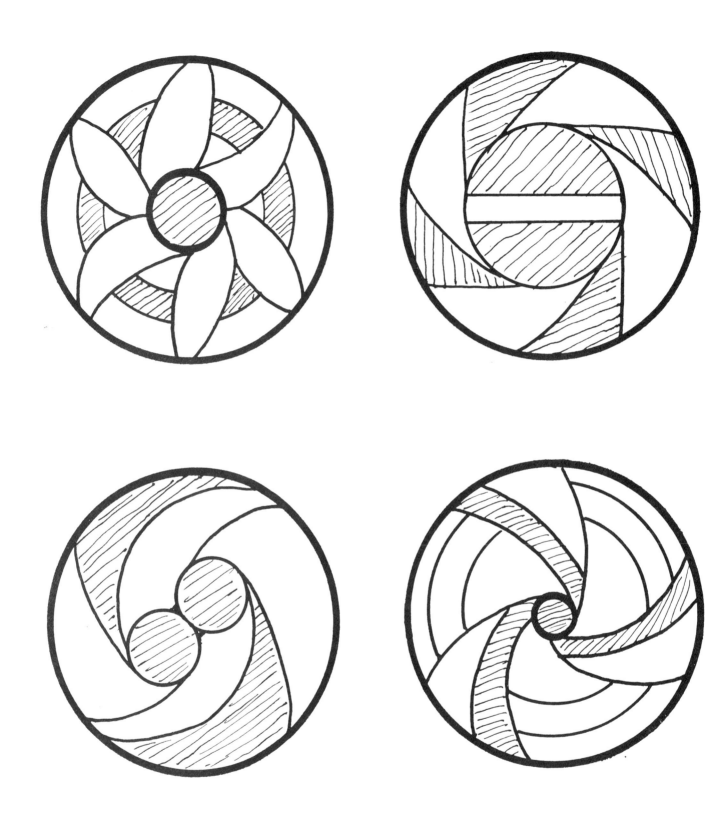

24

27

29

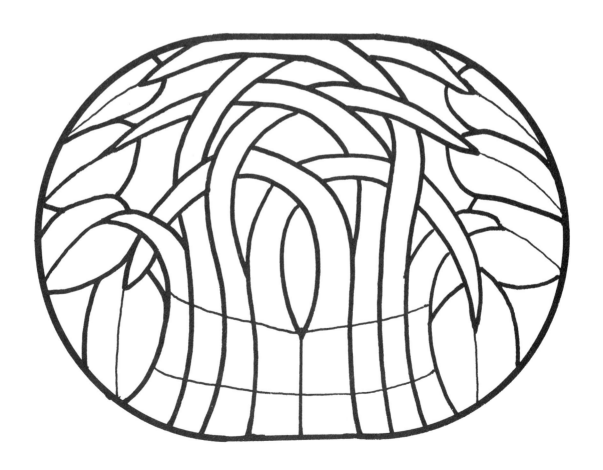

45

49

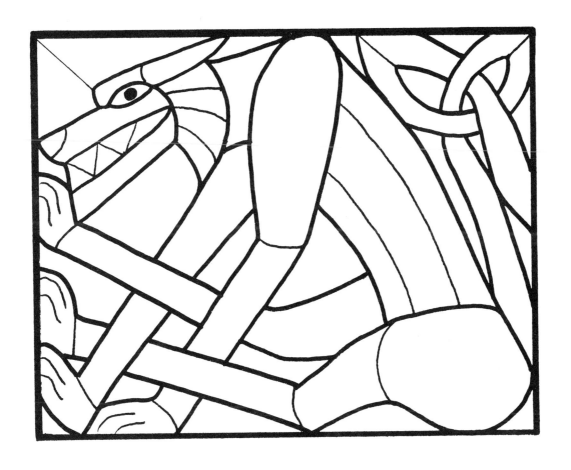

54

St. Mark

St. Matthew

St. John